AF587427

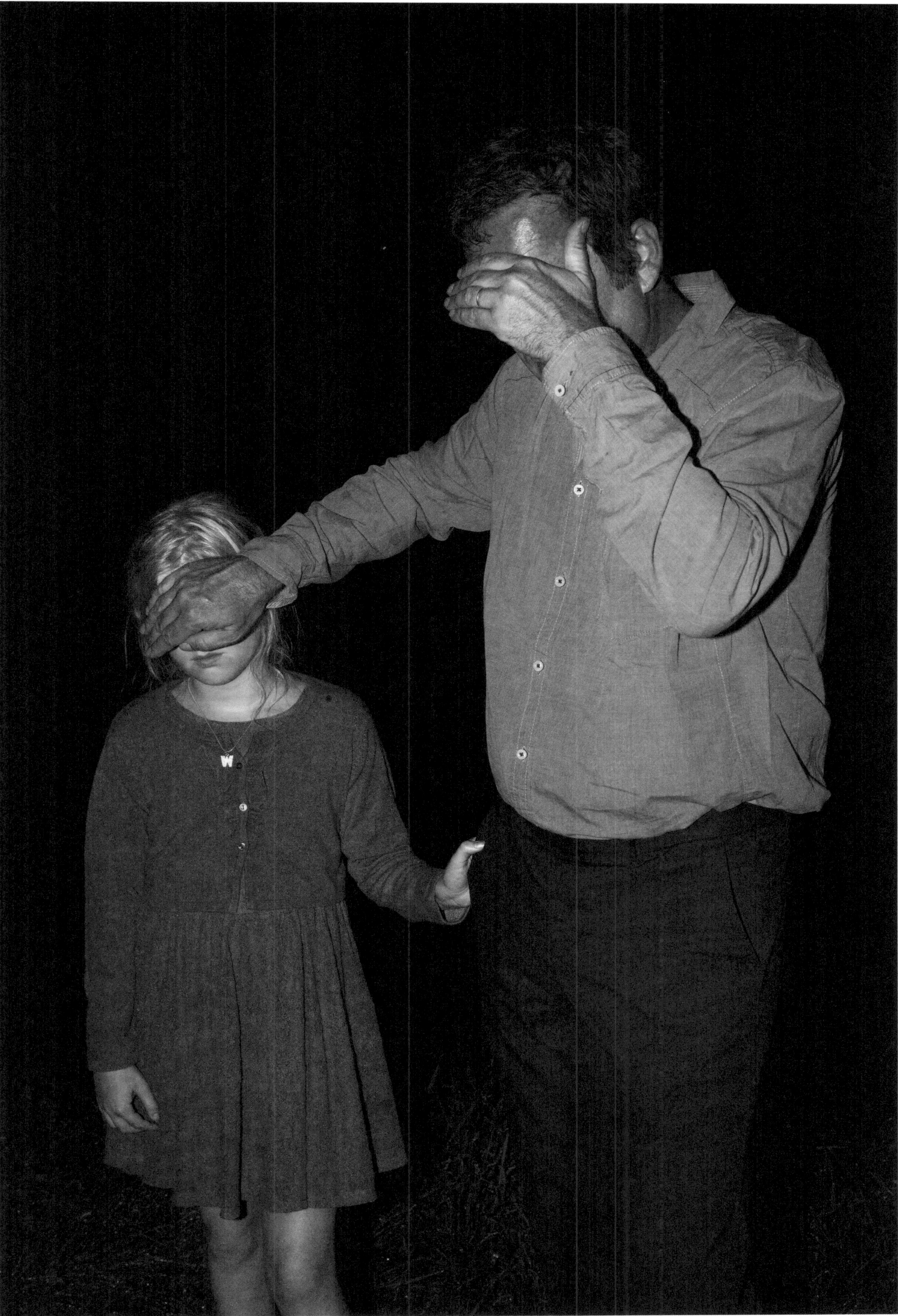

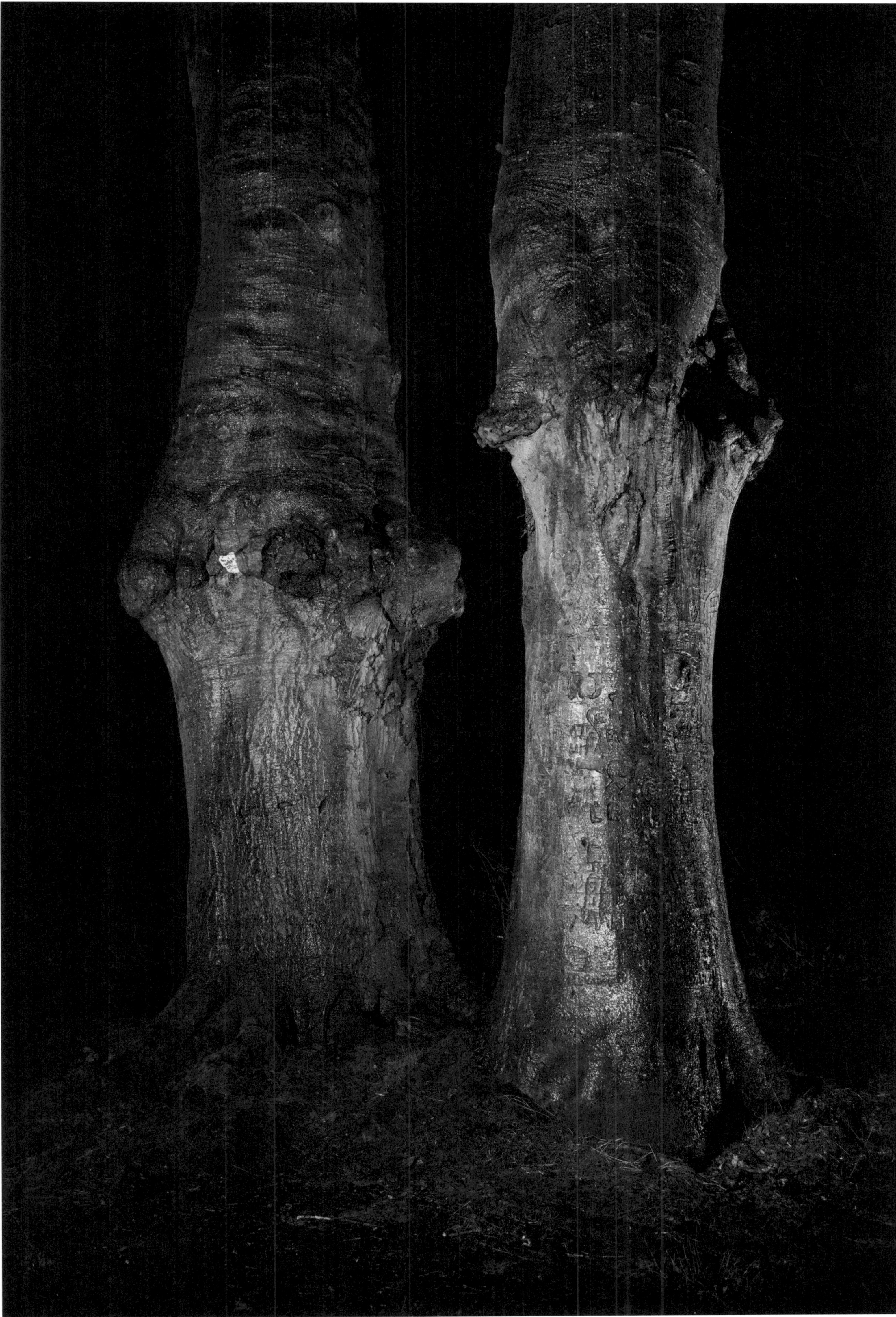

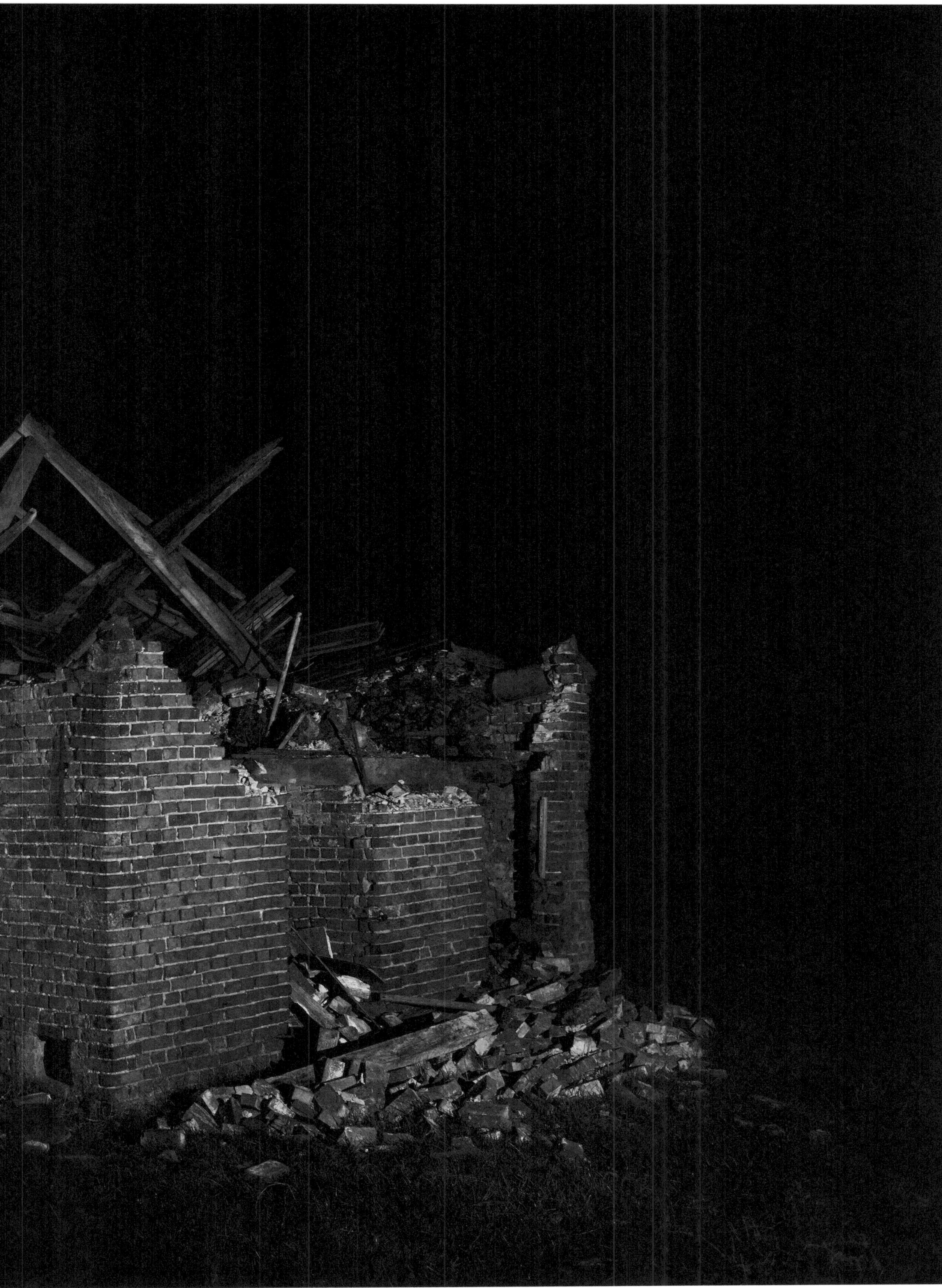

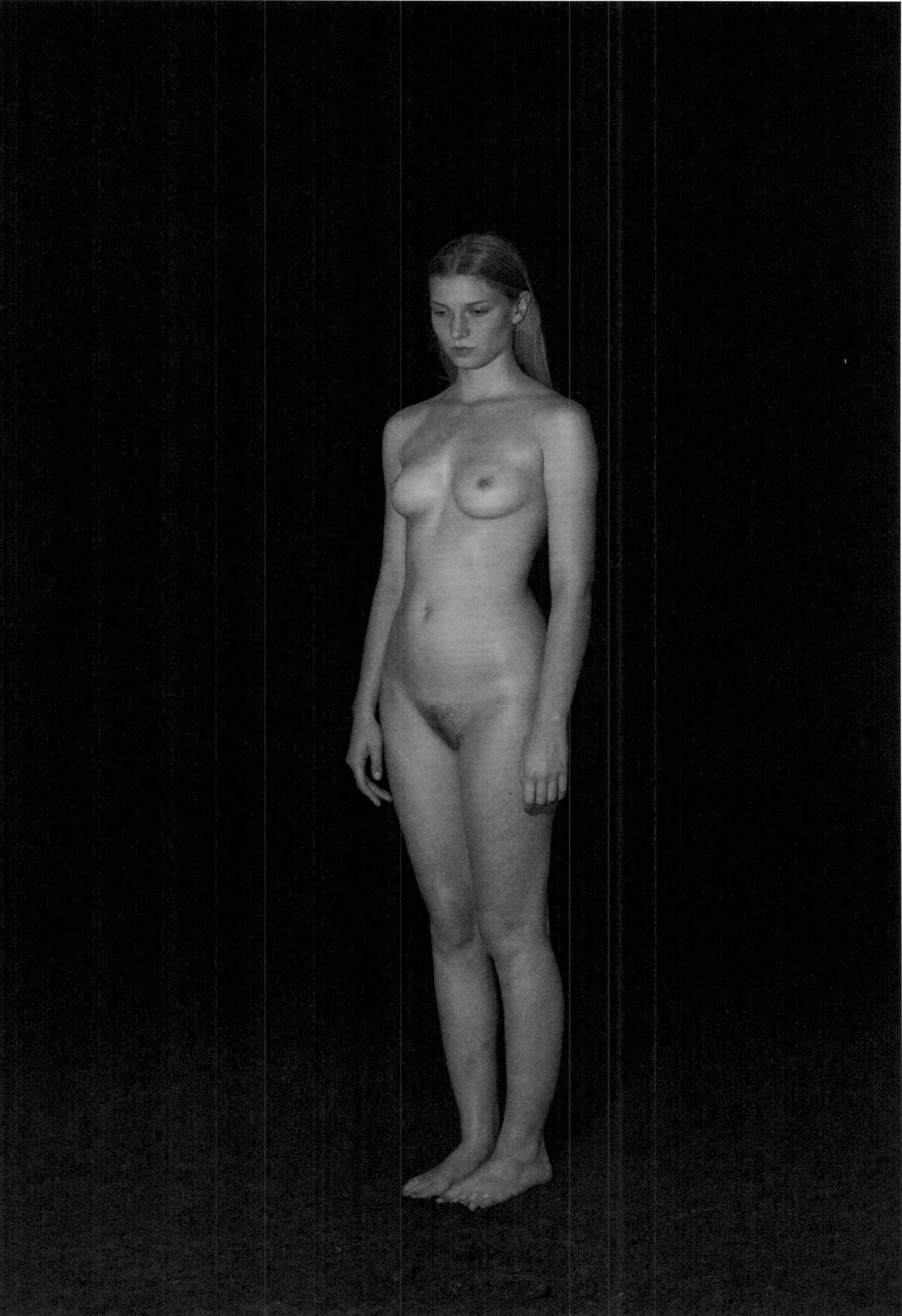

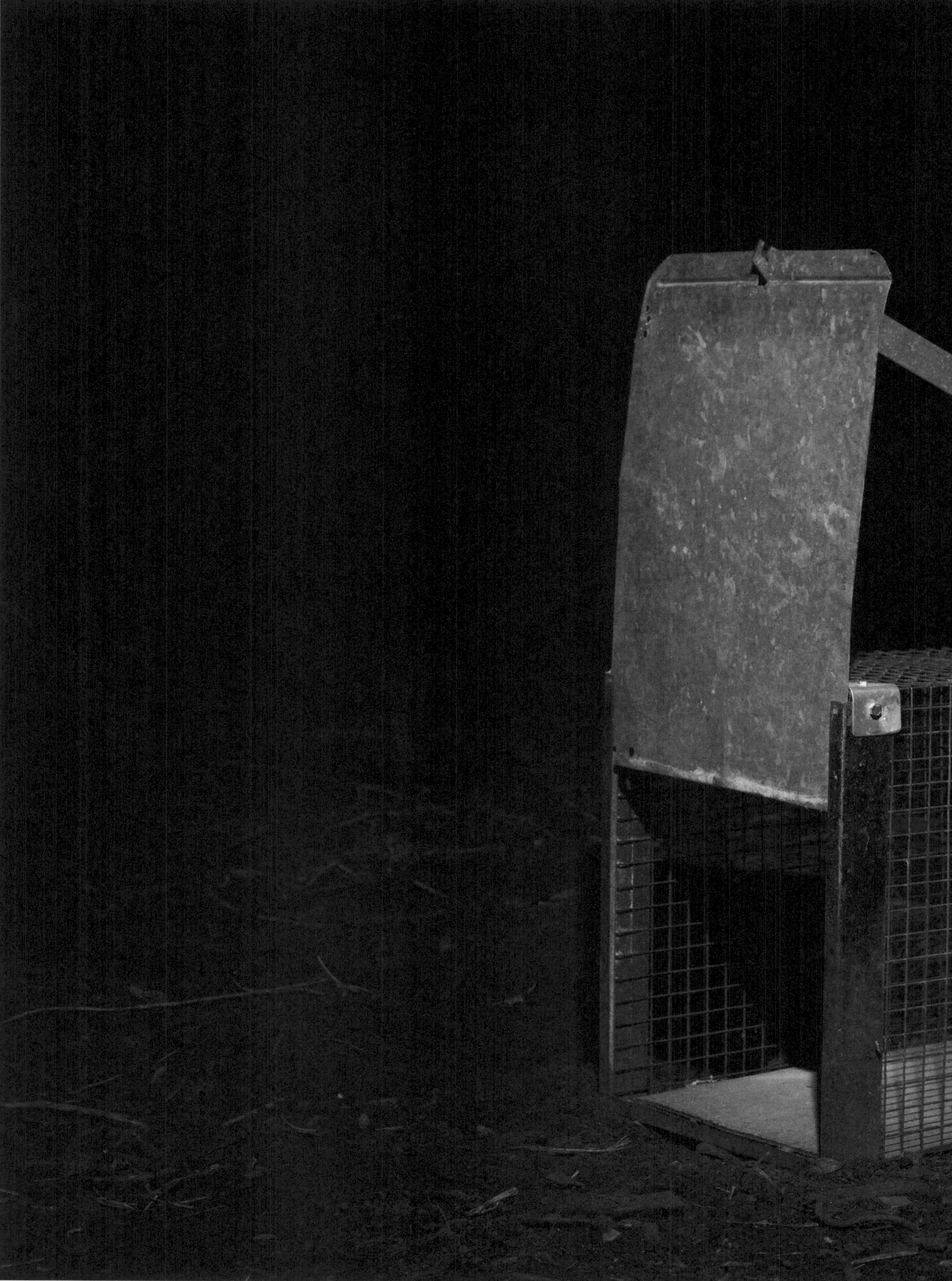

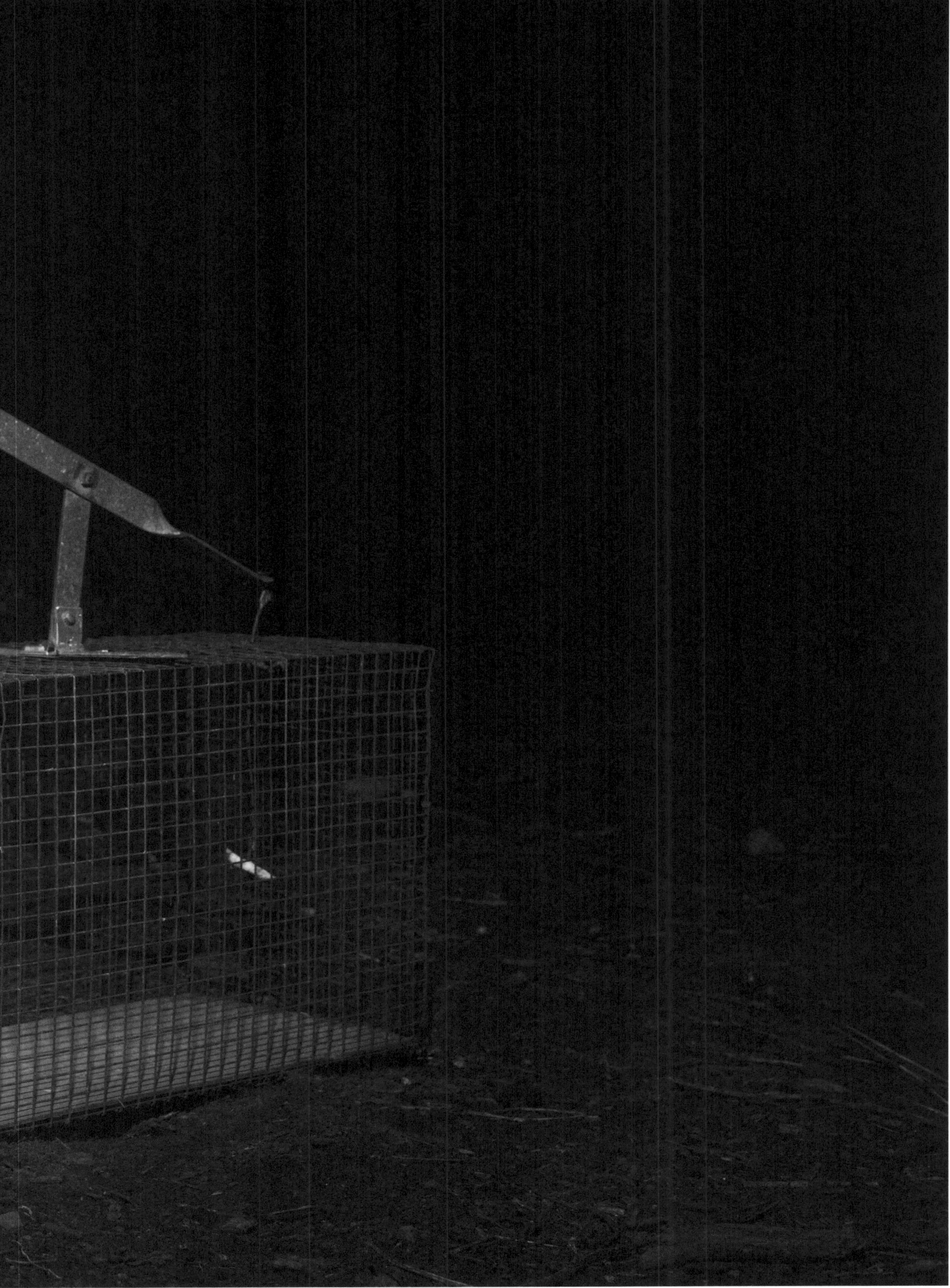

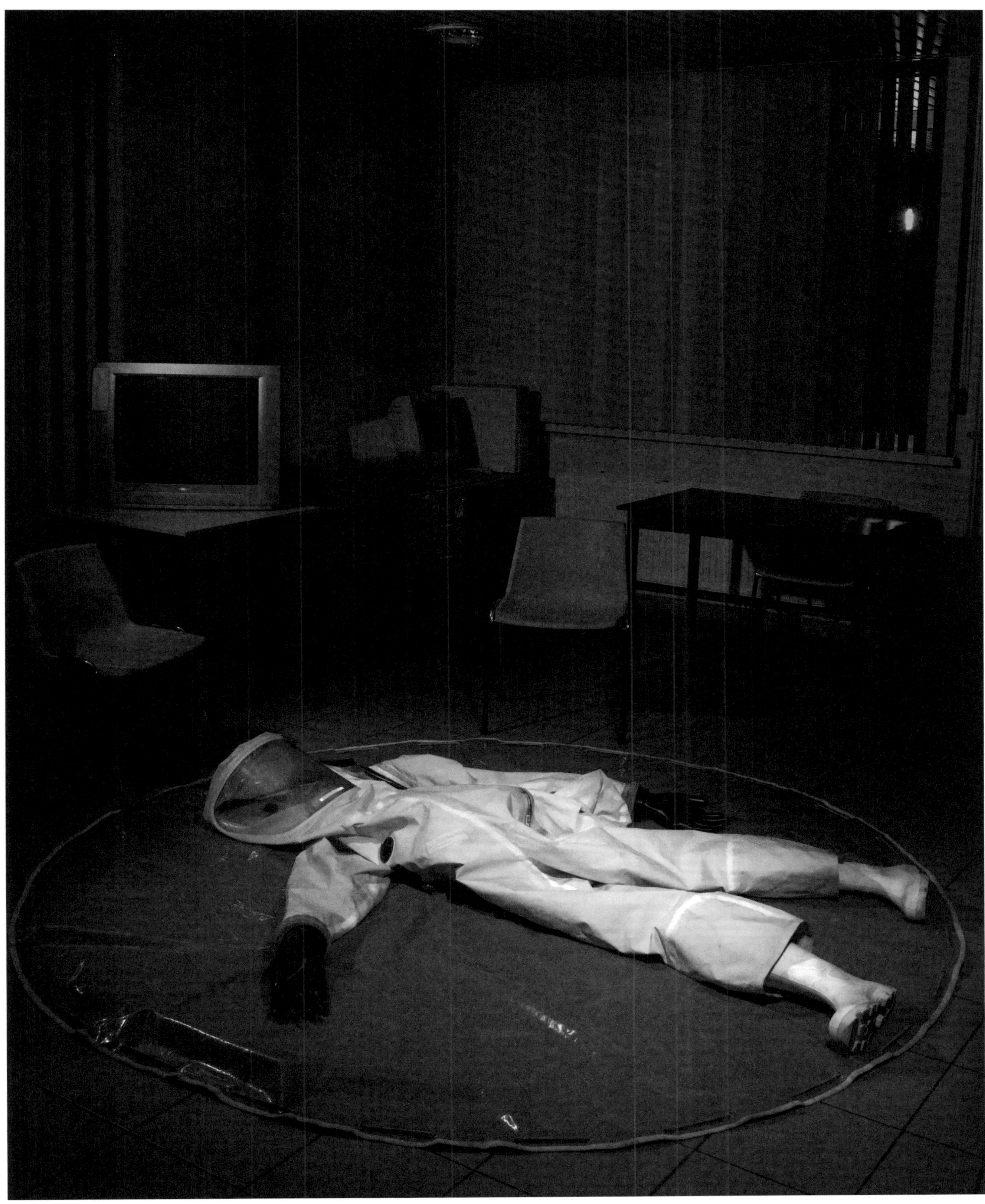

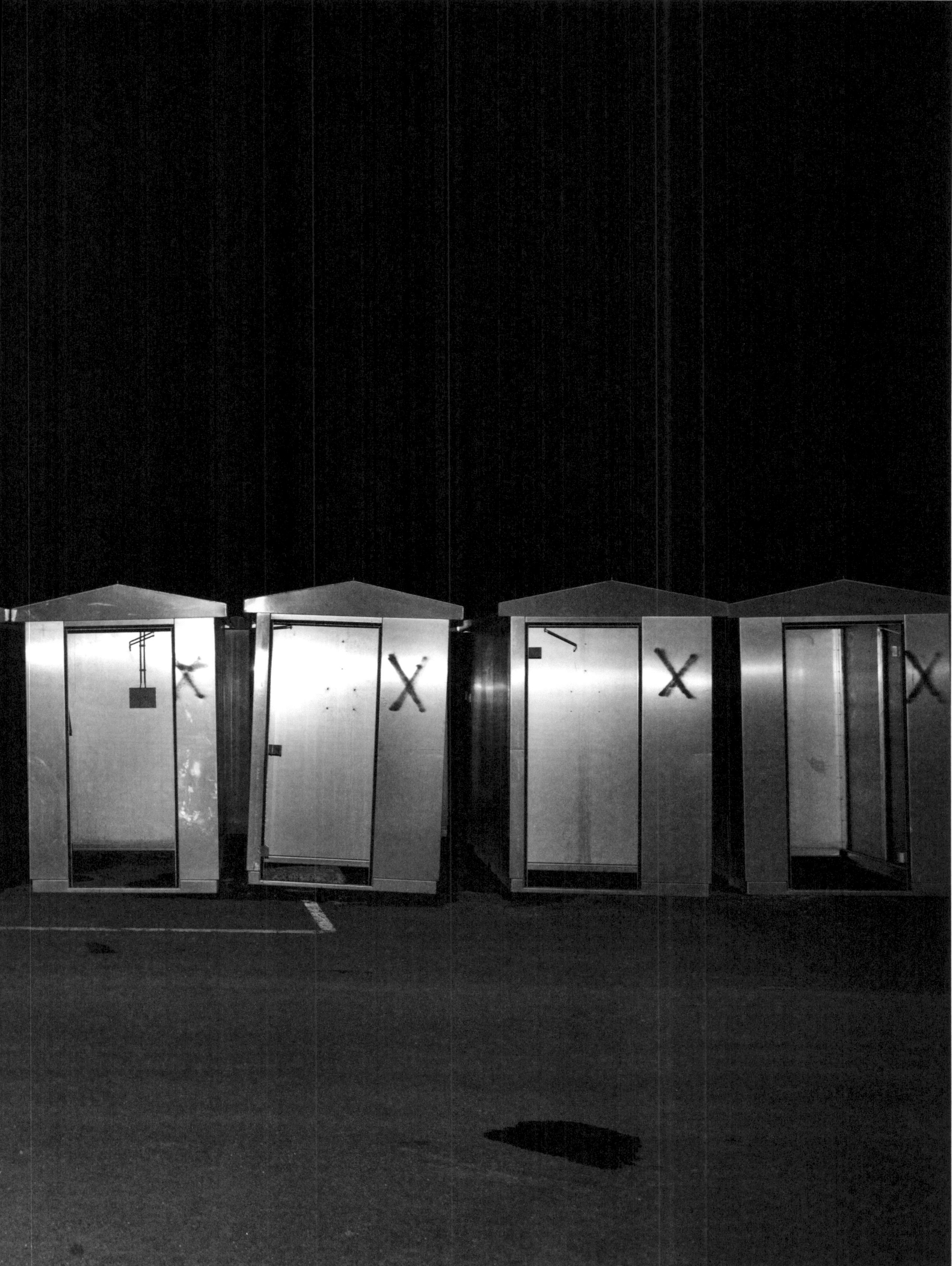

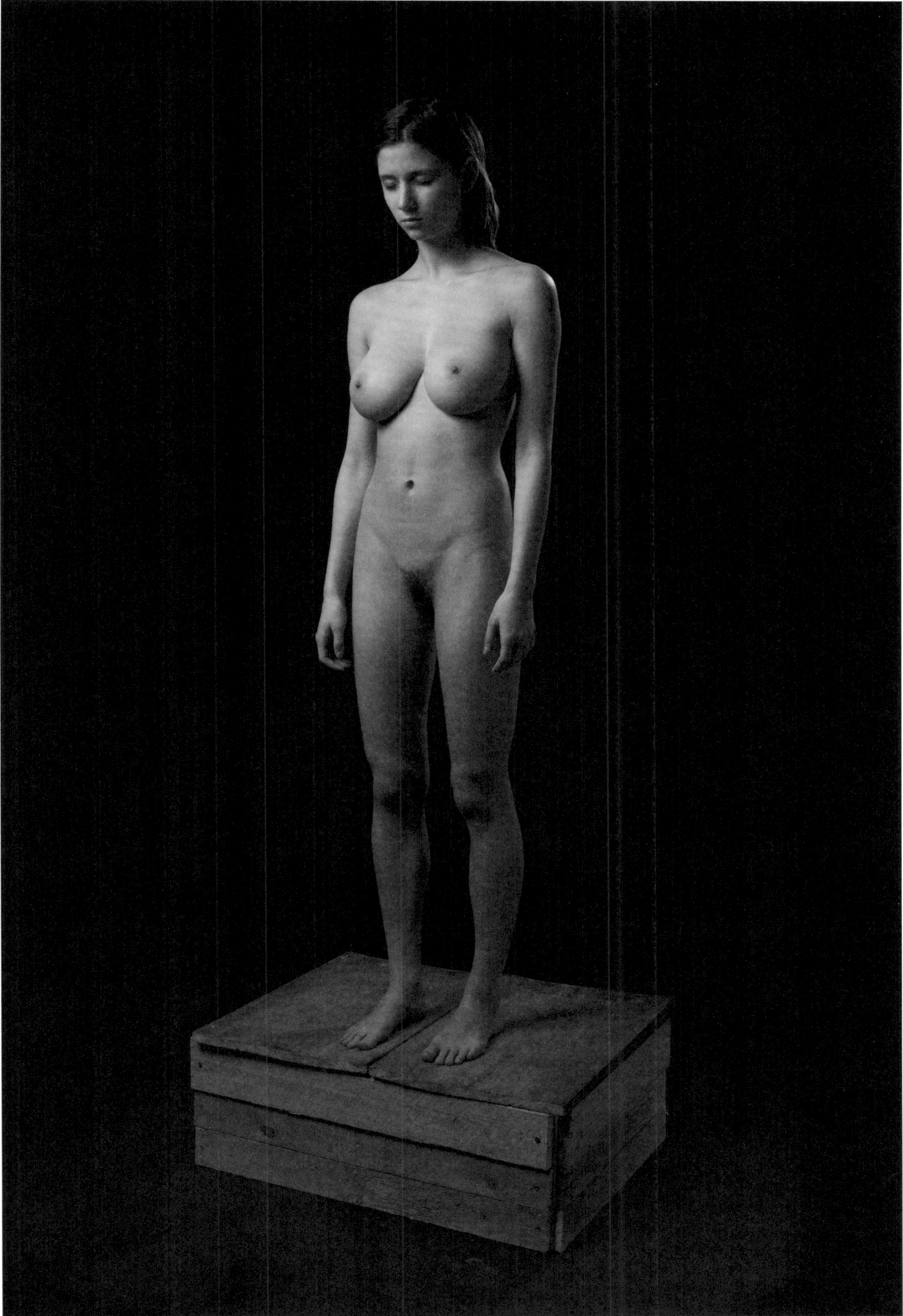

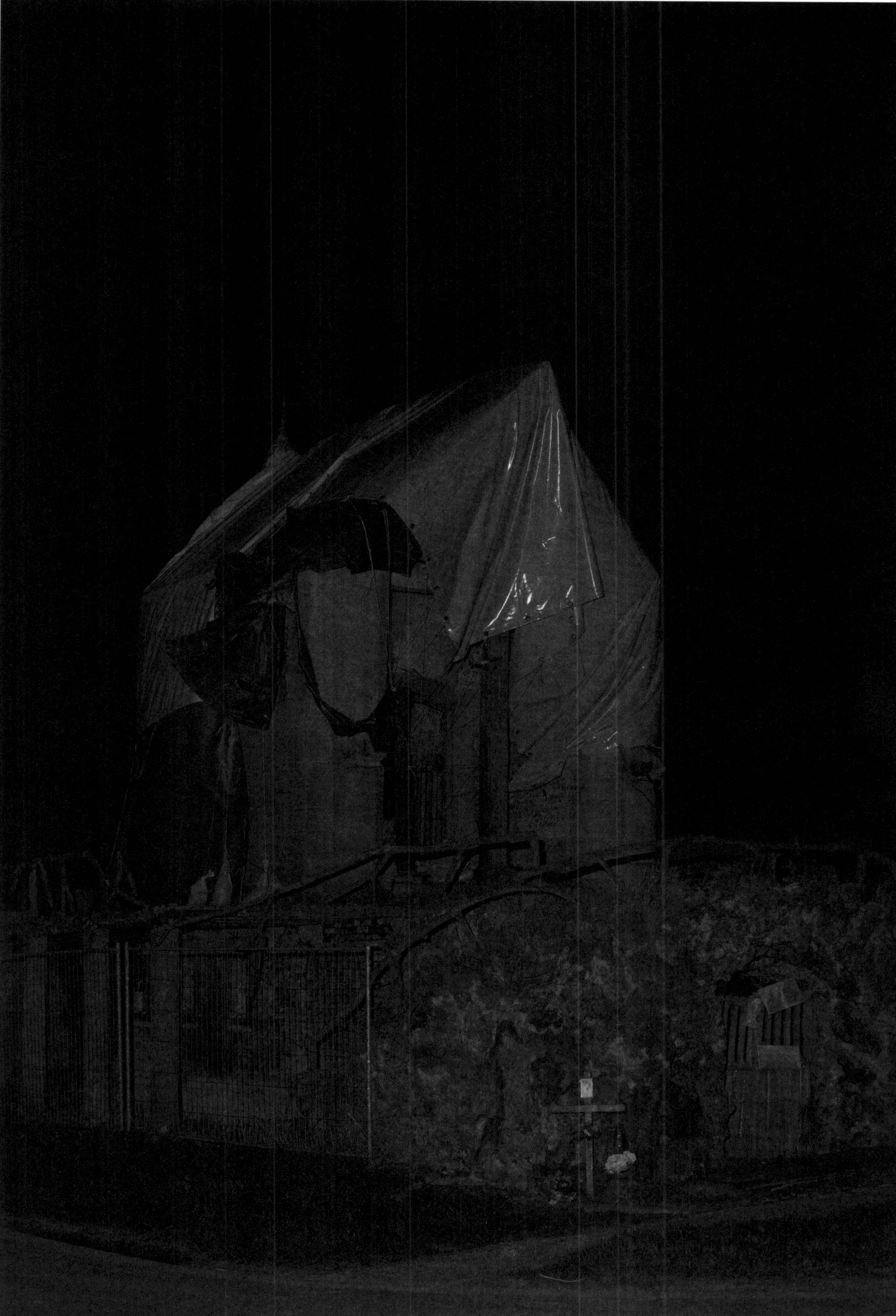

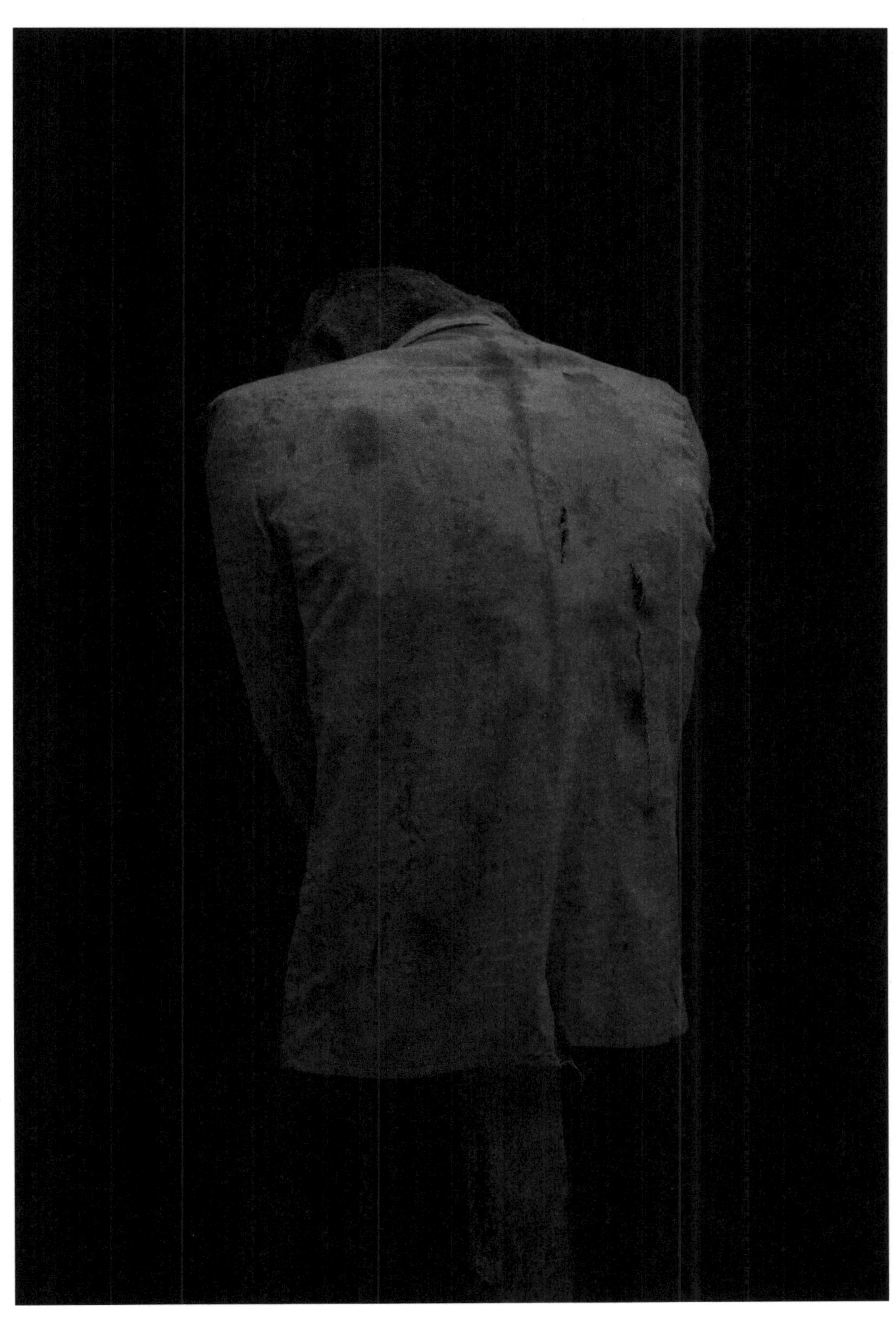

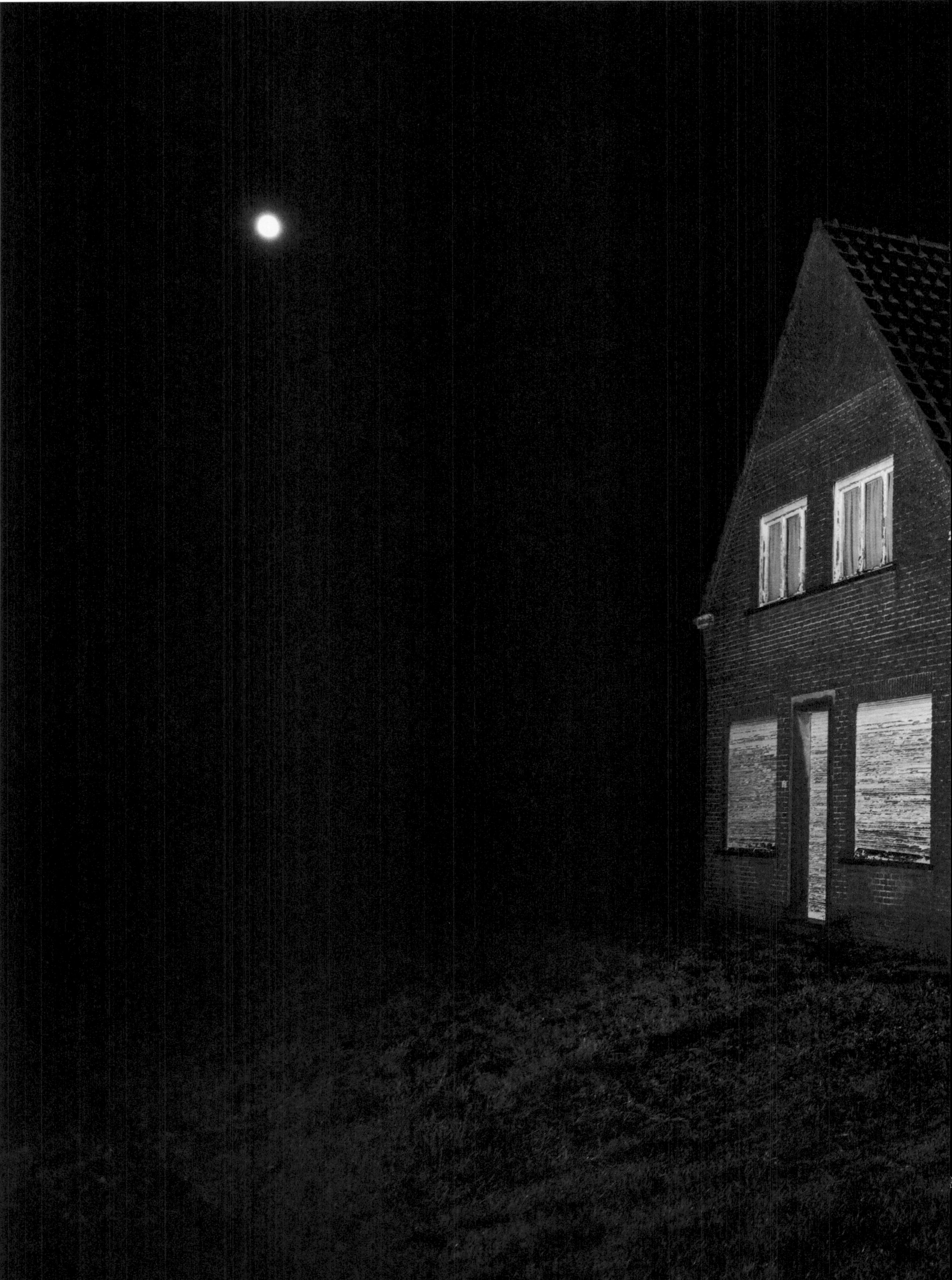

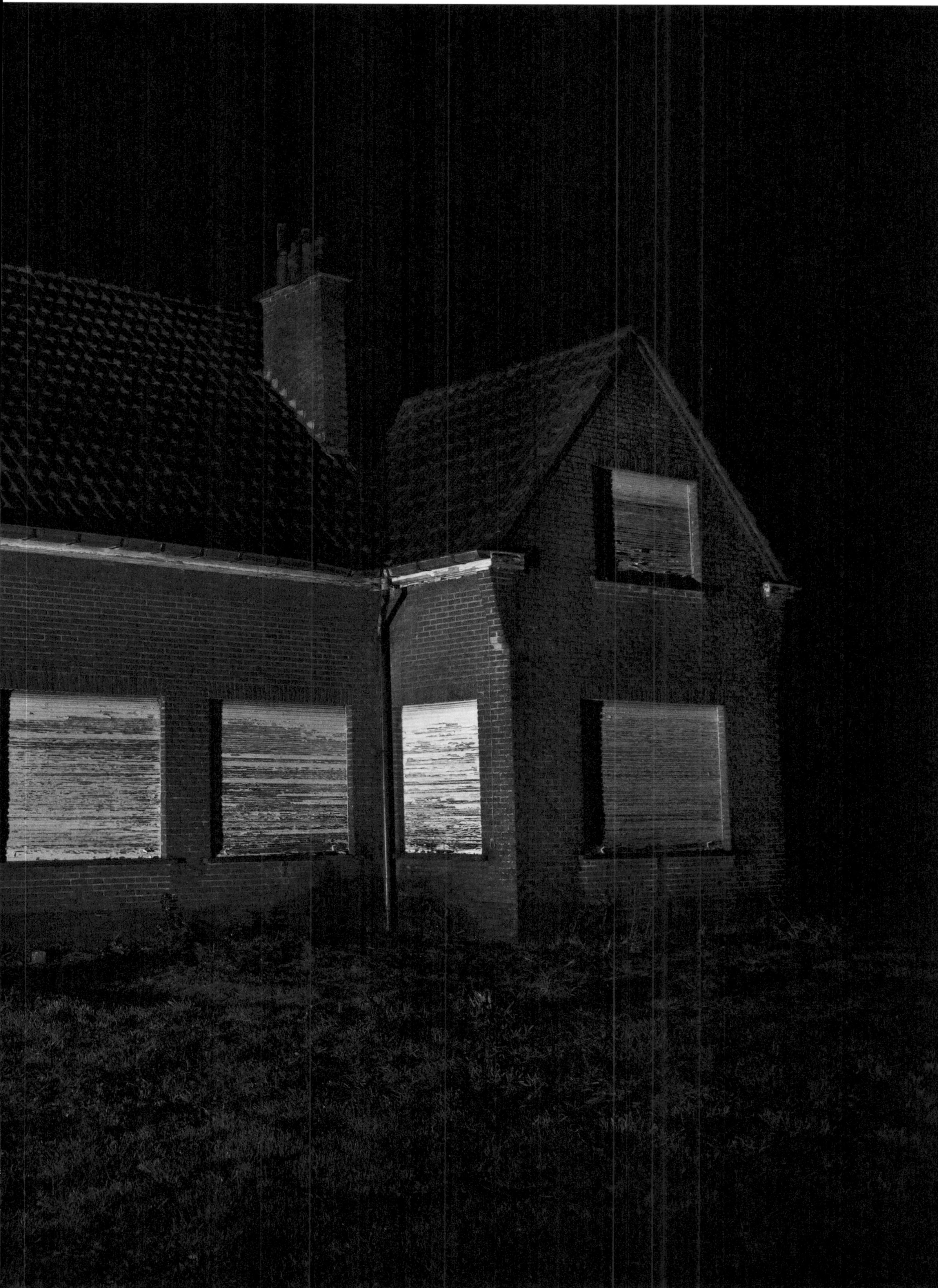

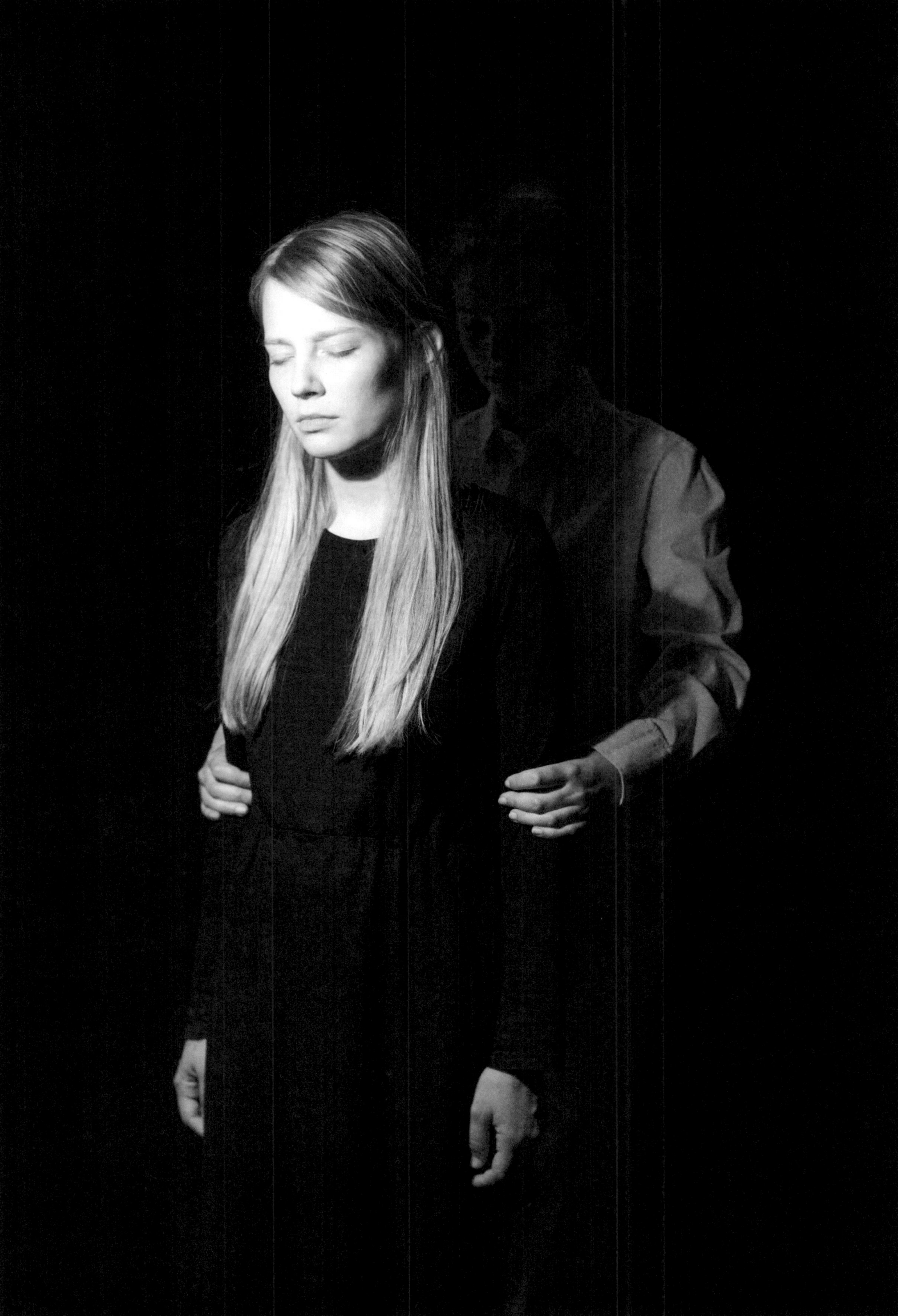

APE#041
Tom Callemin, Hinterland

ISBN 9789490800246
www.artpapereditions.org
www.tomcallemin.be
First edition of 500 copies

Thanks to Hilde, Hans, Annelies,
Anouk, Yves, Esther, Lore, Ludo,
Winde, Stine, Romy

Graphic design: Jurgen Maelfeyt

Print: Die Keure, Bruges